Life Cycles

Squirrels

Julie K. Lundgren

ROURKE PUBLISHING

www.rourkepublishing.com

www.rourkepublishing.com

Photo credits: Cover © Lovely Lita's Sheltering Tree Foundation Inc. squirrel rescue and rehab, JJM, A.Vasilyev; Title Page © Tatiana Grozetskaya; Contents © Chas, imagesbycat, TessarTheTegu; Page 5 © Fidel, Jemini Joseph; Page 6 © aspen rock; Page 7 © Ken Thomas; Page 8 © John Czenke; Page 9 © Fidel; Page 10 © Lovely Lita's Sheltering Tree Foundation Inc. squirrel rescue and rehab; Page 11 © Anne Kitzman; Page 12 © JJM; Page 13 © imagesbycat; Page 14 © Chas; Page 15 © dymon; Page 16 © Arto Hakola; Page 17 © Edd Westmacott; Page 18 © TessarTheTegu; Page 19 © Martha Marks; Page 20 © jeff gynane; Page 21 © Sybille Yates; Page 22 © Lovely Lita's Sheltering Tree Foundation Inc. squirrel rescue and rehab, JJM, Martha Marks

Editor: Jeanne Sturm

Cover and page design by Nicola Stratford, bdpublishing.com

Library of Congress Cataloging-in-Publication Data

Lundgren, Julie K.
 Squirrels / Julie K. Lundgren.
    p. cm.
 Includes bibliographical references and index.
 ISBN 978-1-61590-310-8 (Hard cover) (alk. paper)
 ISBN 978-1-61590-549-2 (Soft cover)
 1. Squirrels--Juvenile literature. I. Title.
 QL737.R68L86 2011
 599.36--dc22
                              2010009027

Rourke Publishing
Printed in the United States of America, North Mankato, Minnesota
033010
033010LP

www.rourkepublishing.com - rourke@rourkepublishing.com
Post Office Box 643328, Vero Beach, Florida 32964

Table of Contents

Climbers and Diggers

Squirrels belong to a group of animals called **mammals**. Like other mammals, squirrels have fur and control their own body temperature. Unlike many other mammals, most squirrels are active during the day, making them easy to watch.

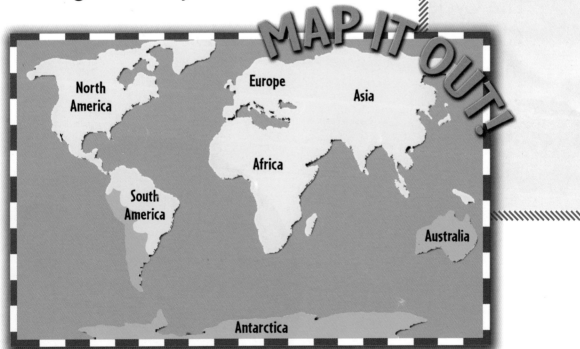

MAP IT OUT!

Squirrels live in grasslands, forests, farms, and towns in most parts of the world, except Antarctica, Australia, and parts of South America.

Eurasian red squirrels, like many tree squirrels, stay active all winter, even on very cold days. Fur and food keep them warm.

Thirteen-lined ground squirrels can be found in central North America. Larger ground squirrels, like the yellow-bellied marmot and the woodchuck, are also common in the United States.

Thirteen-lined ground squirrels have 13 rows of stripes and spots.

Eastern fox squirrels find their food and make their homes in trees.

Flying squirrels come out at night. Their large eyes help them see in the dark.

Scientists divide squirrels into three kinds based on their body shape. Tree squirrels have big, bushy tails and sharp claws. Ground squirrels have strong legs for digging. Flying squirrels have extra skin folds on their sides that allow them to glide through the air for short distances.

DID YOU KNOW?

Sharp claws make tree squirrels excellent climbers. They can even hang by their back feet.

Squirrels eat mainly seeds and nuts. They also munch mushrooms and other **fungi**, bird eggs, tree buds, insects, and very young birds. In early spring, gray squirrels lick the sweet sap that leaks from cracks in the bark of maple trees.

Squirrels have front teeth that never stop growing. Constant chewing shortens and sharpens them.

Tree squirrels often eat up in the safety of trees and drop the shells below. Look for nut shells and pine cone pieces on the ground to find favorite squirrel dining areas.

Cycle Snapshot

Northern flying squirrels also eat **lichens.**

Squirrels **cache** food for winter. To find the buried nuts or seeds again, they sniff and dig. The ones they do not find sprout and become new plants and trees.

Babies

Each of Earth's plants and animals begins, grows, **reproduces**, and dies. This life cycle happens again and again so that life continues. The squirrel life cycle starts when a mother squirrel gives birth to a **litter** of babies.

Helpless newborn squirrels have very little fur and cannot see or hear. For six to eight weeks, they sleep, grow, and drink milk from their mother. They curl around each other to keep warm.

Tree squirrels and flying squirrels make homes in tree hollows or leaf and twig nests.

Cycle Snapshot

All mammal mothers make milk for their babies.

Baby squirrels have sealed eyes and ears at birth. After about two weeks, their ears begin to open. Their eyes open after two to three more weeks.

Baby squirrels, like many other mammals, depend on their mother for food and care. Squirrel fathers do not help. Tree squirrels may have two litters each year. Flying squirrels and many ground squirrels have one litter per year.

At two weeks of age, squirrels have started to grow fur, but their eyes are still sealed.

Older babies, with eyes and ears open and a coat of fur to keep them warm, are ready to explore outside the burrow.

DID YOU KNOW?

Tree squirrels generally have smaller litters than ground squirrels. Tree squirrel mothers may have one to four babies in a litter, while ground squirrels may have as many as nine.

Squirrel School

The young squirrels begin to explore the world outside their nest. They must learn how to climb safely, find food and water, and defend themselves. Squirrels face many dangers.

Tree squirrels use their tails for balance, like a tightrope walker uses a pole.

Tree squirrels hop and leap from place to place.

Tree squirrels run along branches and leap between trees on familiar paths. These tree highways have squirrel **scent marks** on them that help the squirrels easily, quickly, and safely find their way. Their sharp claws grip the bark.

Forest hawks, like this Cooper's hawk, hunt tree squirrels.

Squirrels head for their burrows or the nearest tree when they see dogs or cats come near.

Squirrels face many enemies. Hawks, snakes, dogs, and cats hunt squirrels and their young. Great horned owls sometimes attack leaf and twig nests looking for squirrels. People hunt squirrels, too.

DID YOU KNOW?

Squirrels avoid detection by staying perfectly still and quiet.

To gain skills in climbing, leaping, and defending themselves, young squirrels play together. They discover the best way to break open hard nuts and seeds. At day's end, they pile into the nest and sleep together.

By crunching down in exactly the right place, squirrels crack open nut shells.

Young adult squirrels also begin to learn their place in the squirrel **community**. Older, stronger squirrels are the top bananas and get the best food, homes, and mates.

Young golden-mantled ground squirrel brothers and sisters tumble, chase, and play.

DID YOU KNOW?

Squirrels send messages by chirping, stamping their feet, and waving their tails.

19

Adults

Squirrels reach full size in four to five months. They spend their first winter on their own. When spring comes, they find a partner to begin the cycle again.

Black-tailed prairie dogs, a kind of ground squirrel, weigh 2 to 3 pounds (about 1 kilogram) as adults.

Unlike tree squirrels, many ground squirrels hibernate through the winter.

Cycle Snapshot

Many people set out food for tree squirrels so they can enjoy watching these talented acrobats.

A Front Row Seat

See squirrels up close. Set out dried corn or seeds on the ground, an old stump, or a bird feeder. Birds and squirrels especially like sunflower seeds. These seeds provide plenty of energy.

Life Cycle Round-up

1 Baby squirrels are born. Their ears and eyes are sealed and they have little or no fur.

4 Adults find mates and begin the cycle again.

3 Young squirrels learn to take care of themselves.

2 Baby squirrels drink their mother's milk. They grow fur. Their ears, then eyes, begin to open.

Glossary

cache (KASH): store or hide something for later use

community (kuh-MYU-nuh-tee): a group of animals living in one area

fungi (FUN-gye): plantlike living things that do not flower, like mushrooms

hibernate (HYE-bur-nayt): greatly slow down the body's systems in order to survive poor or cold conditions

lichens (LYE-kenz): flat, colorful living things that grow on trees, rocks, and other flat surfaces and are made up of a fungus and a kind of simple plant living together

litter (LIT-er): a batch of animal babies, all born at the same time from one mother

mammals (MAM-uhlz): a group of animals, including squirrels and people, that make their own heat, have fur or hair, and make milk for their babies

reproduces (ree-pruh-DOOS-ehz): makes more of something

scent marks (SENT MARKS): spots where animals have laid down smelly body oils, as a way to send messages to other animals

Index

Websites to Visit

animal.discovery.com/guides/mammals/habitat/tempforest/eastsquir.html

animaldiversity.ummz.umich.edu/site/accounts/information/Sciuridae.html

www.flyingsquirrels.com/

www.nhptv.org/Natureworks/abertssquirrel.htmprojectsquirrel.org/

www.squirrels.org/

About the Author

Julie K. Lundgren grew up near
Lake Superior where she reveled
in mucking about in the woods, picking
berries, and expanding her rock collection.
Her appetite for learning about nature led
her to a degree in biology from
the University of Minnesota.
She currently lives in Minnesota with
her husband and two sons.